I0569343

Printed in the United States of America

Michael J. Gaetke and our logos are trademarks of Michael J. Gaetke

YesGodAdventure.org

619.736.0233

In partnership with

 Goodwill Media Services,Corp.

www.goodwillmediaservices.com

105 Macclamrock Ct.
Cary, NC 27518

Kindle Store> Kindle ebooks>Religion & Spirituality> Christian Books & Bibles> Ministry & Evangelism

Paperback ISBN: 979-8-9913145-1-0
Hardback ISBN: 979-8-9913145-0-3
eBook ISBN: 979-8-9913145-2-7

MICHAEL J. GAETKE

SAY
YES
TO
GOD

The Story of an Ordinary Life
of Extraordinary Adventure

Say Yes To God

The Story of an Ordinary Life of Extraordinary Adventure

Michael J. Gaetke

2024 © by Michael J. Gaetke

All rights reserved. Published 2024.

No part of this publication may be reproduced or transmitted in any form or by any means, electronic or mechanical, including photocopying, recording, or any information storage and retrieval system now known or yet to be invented, without written permission from the publisher, except in cases of brief quotations in critical articles and reviews.

BIBLE SCRIPTURES

Scriptures taken from the Holy Bible, New International Version®, NIV®. Copyright © 1973, 1978, 1984, 2011 by Biblica, Inc.™ Used by permission of Zondervan. All rights reserved worldwide. www.zondervan.com The "NIV" and "New International Version" are trademarks registered in the United States Patent and Trademark ™.Office by Biblica, Inc

DEDICATION

I dedicate this book, my story, to my incredible partner in adventure, Cathy, my wonderful wife. I also dedicate it to my beloved children and grandchildren: David and his wife Emily, Nicole, Paul, Eloise, and Margot. You all bring me immense joy, and I cherish every moment of our family adventures together!

CONTENTS

Foreword

Are you an adventurous person? I don't mean an Indiana Jones kind of adventure, but a real one—the kind where you wake up and realize it wasn't a dream or a movie script. Your life and mine are meant to be lived fully, but let's be honest: when we consider the realities of paying a mortgage, raising kids, going to work, and sneaking in a few minutes of quiet and relaxation, it's all good—but it's all-consuming too, right? We can end up thinking, "Where does my life have time for adventure?"

It's all about perspective. The important question is: How do you see your life? Do you see it as a small part of a big world and doubt the significance of your role? Or is there something bigger going on—something greater than the limitations of the natural world, possibly even something supernatural? Does your perspective include the possibility of a divine partnership?

The idea of a divine partnership with a holy, perfect, and all-powerful God is mind-blowing. Yet, that is precisely what God promises those who follow Him by faith. Yes, it does require faith. However, it's not a blind leap but the kind of trust you find in your soul that allows you to know you are deeply loved and cared for by someone who will never let you down.

You can be on adventures in faraway and exotic places, but sometimes your great adventures are right where you live. Either way, they happen when you start saying "yes" to God. I asked you if you were an adventurous person. I'll be candid with you, I'm not naturally adventurous. But I find my life to be extraordinary because, like Mike Gaetke, the author of this book, I partner with God.

Saying "yes" to God isn't about duty or drudgery. It does involve obedience, but it's the kind of obedience that sets you free to see your life as an adventure filled with both ups and downs, always bringing a sense of peace to your soul—something elusive to many today.

Saying "yes" to God captures, in the purest sense, a leaning into becoming the person God designed you to be. I've known Mike for more than thirty-five years, and he's the real deal. A gifted and godly man, good friend, successful leader and businessman, great dad, and husband who humbly considers himself to be ordinary. But I can promise you his life is extraordinary, as you will soon read in the pages of this book.

Partnerships are important, like Mike's partnership (marriage) with his wife Cathy. She's an amazing human being who loves others well and is loved in return. Mike and Cathy together are a kind and unassuming couple, yet truly a Kingdom force to be reckoned with. You may have a significant partnership too, maybe in business, but there is nothing that compares to the divine partnership where God does His part and you do yours.

Your adventure with God may or may not be in faraway places that bring amazing stories, and many times they are not grand or glamorous. The real measure is about results and relationships. This includes the impact of eternal value (changed lives) that becomes part of your personal legacy, along with the significance of meaningful relationships with those with whom you enjoy your life. Isn't that the adventure we all desire?

This book will stir your mind, encourage your soul, and challenge your life to be bigger than you have dreamed it to be—if you say "yes" to God.

-Dan Reiland, Executive Pastor of 12Stone Church

LETTER TO
THE READER

I've had the idea for this book bouncing around in my head for years now, fueled by conversations with friends and the realization that what I've experienced in my walk with God is available to anyone who seeks it. My goal in writing this book is to lead you to a deep understanding: your life has significance. Your life has meaning. By connecting with your Creator and understanding His purpose for your existence, everything can change. You can experience an ordinary life of extraordinary adventure!

If you view your Christianity as a footnote to your life rather than its center, you are missing out on the best parts of the Christian "life to the fullest" that God offers us. We can go to church, do all the right things, check all the boxes, and try our best to be 'good,' but that still won't be enough. To really experience all that God has for you, the Christian life has to be your whole life. Your relationship with Christ must be the focus, and without a doubt, that is truly the best way to live!

Another big thing I've experienced is that sometimes we come across opportunities that God puts in our life's path, and our default reaction is to hesitate or doubt. We put them in the "no" column or decide not to do them before we have truly considered them, even if we want to say "yes." These could be fears about lack of time, lack of money, fear of failing, worrying about what others will think, feeling like you are not qualified, or not being able to see what God might want to do through us. Maybe you have felt that way before. But you know what? We can overcome these fears if we start with a "yes" attitude. Yes, we'll have fears, but let's give them to Jesus before we let them hold us back. Let's take the opportunities He gives us and go with them until He says otherwise. I like to state it this way: "When God provides an opportunity, start with 'yes' until God gives you a compelling 'no.'" This is the beginning of an ordinary life of extraordinary adventure!

When you make this switch in the way you think, your life can transition from confusion and desperation to one filled with purpose, meaning, and adventure. This is why I wrote this book—for you—because of God's profound love for you and His desire for you to experience real life. Walking with God transforms life from a mere journey to an extraordinary adventure filled with purpose, joy, and countless blessings waiting to be discovered. So, buckle up, say "yes" to adventure, and get ready for the ride of a lifetime.

INTRODUCTION

Imagine finding yourself navigating the dense, humid jungle of Papua New Guinea on a Saturday morning, surrounded by the earthy scent of vegetation and the surround sound of wildlife. That's exactly where I was, accompanied by Windi, a local friend who had invited me to visit his remote village and meet his father. Without hesitation, I accepted the opportunity.

Our journey began with a rough ride on a four-wheeler until the road ended. Then, we walked for another three or four hours through the jungle until we reached his remote village.

When we arrived, the little kids who were there saw me, screamed, and ran away. I asked, "What's going on? Why are they so upset?" He explained, "They've never seen a white man before. You're the first white man that's ever been to this village." I can't imagine what they thought when they saw me!

Windi's father was really excited to see us when we arrived. We did their ceremonial introductions, and he announced, "We're going to have a feast!" We entered a small, one-room house made of woven bamboo walls and a thatched roof, with a fire in the middle of the room. His father brought a pig inside, put it in a headlock, and beat its head with a rock until it was dead. Then, he rolled the pig around on the fire to burn the hair off and started butchering it with a bamboo knife. I will never forget the awful smell of the hair burning off that pig! After the pig was prepped, they wrapped up portions with banana leaves, sweet potatoes, greens, and veggies, then tossed it all into a pit with hot coals and buried it. By then, it was around 10 at night, and we were ready to hit the hay.

We bunked down in the house—guys on one side, girls on the other. There were about eight or ten of us sleeping on smashed bamboo mats laid over the dirt floor, and I could feel bugs crawling all around us and on me. Just as I started to fall asleep, the villagers came in and said the food was ready. It was now mealtime, but note, it was truly the middle of the night. They had a different sense of time, just doing things when they were ready.

So, at three in the morning, we all woke up excited for the feast. The father cut out the pig's liver and put it on a fresh banana leaf, along with some sweet potato and greens, and handed it to me. Not being a big liver fan, I asked if I could offer it back to him out of respect. But my friend Windi said, nope, I had to eat it as the honored guest first before anyone else could. So, that's what I did. Honestly, I'm not even sure if I chewed it or just swallowed it whole.

After the meal, we spent the day exploring the village. It was a fantastic experience. What struck me was how Windi's father welcomed us without any prior notice. He just wanted to give his best, no hesitation. It was incredibly humbling to see their generosity, even though they seemed to have so little. It was an adventure I wouldn't have had if I hadn't said "yes" to God.

Honestly, I could write a whole separate book just on my Papua New Guinea adventures, but that is not the point of this book. Possibly, that will be my next book project!

So, how did I end up in the middle of the jungle eating pig liver? To answer that, let's go back in time.

PART ONE

Foundations of Faith

CHAPTER ONE

SAY YES TO GOD: ORDINARY LIFE, EXTRAORDINARY ADVENTURE

"I'm no one special, but I serve a special God!"
– Michael J. Gaetke

Life has a funny way of making us feel like we're not up to much, doesn't it? We've all been there, feeling like our contributions might not matter in the big picture. Trust me, you're not alone in this.

Think back to those incredible tales of faith and bravery in the Bible. The folks we read about there? They weren't always brimming with confidence. A lot of them wrestled with doubts and felt like they were falling short.

I remember a moment from my own childhood that really hit me hard with those same feelings. As a child, I was painfully shy and unsure of myself. I must've been around seven or eight, and I had to give an oral book report in front of my whole class. The thought of standing up there and speaking was terrifying. Each time a classmate went up, my anxiety grew. When my turn came, I walked to the front, froze, and couldn't say a single word. Time seemed to stop, and I felt utterly helpless. Eventually, my teacher let me sit down, but the sense of failure stuck with me. I felt so low and helpless to change. How could I get beyond this lack of confidence and shyness?

Around that time, a wise and trusted Sunday School teacher shared a verse that changed my life: 2 Timothy 1:7 (YLT): "For God did not give us a spirit of fear, but of power, and of love, and of a sound mind." That verse became my life anchor, and it continues to bring me comfort to this day. I believe God has fulfilled this verse in my life, and although I am still a fairly reserved person, I am no longer shy at all. Another verse I learned around the same time and have claimed for my life is James 1:5 (NIV): "If any of you lacks wisdom, you should ask God, who gives generously to all without finding fault, and it will be given to you. But when you ask, you must believe and not doubt, because the one who doubts is like a wave of the sea, blown and tossed by the wind." Free wisdom from God! I said, "Sign me up for some of that!" I have often prayed for God's wisdom in my life from that time to today.

Let's go back to those Bible stories. Despite their doubts and insecurities, these ordinary folks trusted in God's plan and said "yes" to His call. Take Moses, for example. When God asked him to lead the Israelites out of Egypt, Moses was full of self-doubt. He wasn't a great speaker and even tried to convince God to pick someone else. But God reassured Moses, promising to be with him and giving him signs to prove His power. Moses finally stepped up, and with God's help, performed miraculous signs, like turning a staff into a snake, parting the Red Sea, and bringing water from a rock. He led the Israelites out of slavery and received the Ten Commandments, guiding them toward the Promised Land (Exodus 3:1-4:17).

Then there's Mary. Imagine being a young girl, probably just a teenager, in a small town when the angel Gabriel appeared to her with astounding news. She was chosen to be the mother of Jesus, the Son of God. Despite her initial shock and questions about how this could happen, Mary accepted God's plan with humility and faith. Mary's obedience and willingness to embrace her extraordinary role changed the course of history (Luke 1:26-38).

David started as a humble shepherd, the youngest of his brothers, seemingly the least likely to become anything great. But when the prophet Samuel came to anoint a new king, God chose David for his heart, not his appearance. David's faith and courage carried him through when he faced Goliath, the giant Philistine warrior. Armed only with a sling and five smooth stones, David declared that the battle belonged to the Lord and defeated Goliath with a single stone to the forehead. This victory marked the beginning of his rise to become a great king of Israel, uniting the nation and establishing Jerusalem as its capital (1 Samuel 16:1-13, 17:1-50).

And then there's Paul, originally known as Saul, who was a fierce persecutor of Christians. He was present at the stoning of Stephen, one of the first Christian martyrs. But on his way to Damascus to arrest more Christians, he had a life-changing encounter with the risen Jesus. A bright light from heaven blinded him, and he heard Jesus' voice asking why he was persecuting Him. After three days of blindness and reflection, Ananias, a disciple, was sent by God to heal and baptize Saul. Renamed Paul, he became one of the most passionate apostles, traveling extensively, preaching the Gospel, and writing many letters that form a significant part of the New Testament (Acts 9:1-19).

These stories show the incredible power of saying "yes" to God's call and trusting His plan. God gave each one of these people just what was needed to go beyond themselves to accomplish and experience amazing miracles and awesome adventures! Through their faith and obedience, these individuals accomplished amazing things and became instruments of His purpose. So, if you ever doubt whether God can use you for something remarkable, remember this: if God could use a shepherd boy, a young girl, and a persecutor of Christians, He can most certainly use you too! It's not about having all the right skills or talents. It's about realizing you don't have within yourself what is needed; it's about having a willing and yielded heart and being open to God's guidance. When you say "yes" to God, you invite Him to work through you in ways you never imagined possible. God has a life of adventure planned for each one of us!

CHAPTER TWO

MY "YES" TO JESUS

"Without God, life has no purpose. And without purpose, life has no meaning." – Rick Warren

Looking back, my faith journey started really young. I probably first prayed to accept Jesus when I was around three or four, or at least that's what my folks told me. But the memory that sticks with me is from a junior high youth camp when I was 13. The speaker asked us if we wanted to leave our old life behind and start fresh with Jesus. We had to come up to the campfire, grab a stick of wood to represent our old life, and throw it into the fire. That was the moment I truly committed to following Jesus.

Before camp, I always considered myself a Christian, growing up in a church-going family and all that. But it was more like something I did because it was part of my upbringing, not something I really owned. I think God knew I needed a moment to step up and say, "This is who I am, this is what I believe, and this is how I want to live my life."

That camp experience was crucial for me. It wasn't like my life was out of control or anything, but my faith wasn't really my own. After that camp, things changed. I started looking at my interactions with others through a different lens, thinking about how I could share the joy and excitement of having God in my life with them.

I also began seeking out ways to get involved in ministry and do things with eternal value. There was a definite shift in how I thought about my faith and my life. I realized that you start your faith journey at some point, and there's so much to learn, but God meets you where you are and puts the right opportunities in front of you.

It's about being faithful in the small things. At first, it was simple stuff like inviting a friend to youth group. But over time, these opportunities grew. Now, here I am, newly returned from a trip to Kenya to teach and speak at a graduation dinner for people who completed the Africa Servant Leader course. If you'd told me back when I decided to really own my faith that I'd be doing something like this, I would've thought it was only for "big" people that God uses, not someone like me.

It's crazy to think about how far God has taken me—from inviting a friend to my youth group to speaking at a servant leader graduation in Kenya 40 years later, and literally participating in Kingdom adventures around the world! It's kind of a crazy thing!

CHAPTER THREE

A FAMILY LEGACY

**"Unless the Lord builds the house, the builders
labor in vain." – Psalm 127:1 (NIV)**

Growing up, my parents were genuine believers and heavily
involved in ministry. We always had people over during the
holidays who had no place to go, and my mom would pack our house
with kids for Bible stories and games. We also sang at retirement
centers and missions, and my grandpa, who was a vocational pastor
in Los Angeles, had us helping out at the Los Angeles Mission
too. These experiences taught me a lot about serving others and
prioritizing what truly matters.

*"When we leave this world for a better home someday, the only
thing we will take with us are the things we gave away." — Derric
Johnson*

Prayer was a big deal in our house. Every night, our family of five:
Dad, Mom, my brother mark, my sister Melody, and myself, would
kneel at this old blue couch and pray for all sorts of things, especially

missionaries. This was back in the 60s, so we'd send care packages and handwritten letters since there was no internet. It made us feel connected to the work God was doing around the world.

Evenings were spent listening to stories and radio programs together. We loved the "Sugar Creek Gang" adventures and the "Unshackled" radio program, which shared stories of people whose lives were transformed by faith in Jesus. Those stories made a big impact on us and kept faith at the center of our lives.

In high school, my social life revolved around church. Our youth group was super active, with choir, ensemble groups, tours, and lots of fun activities. This strong foundation helped me through a brief rebellious phase when I tried some things that didn't align with my values. But I quickly realized that wasn't for me and went back to the values I grew up with. I learned what the world offered was a false version of what I found to be real with a relationship with Jesus. The choice to wholeheartedly follow Jesus after that was a "no-brainer."

My three kids had a similar upbringing. They went on mission trips with me and got involved in church activities. Today, they're all believers in their 30s, following the same path of faith and yielding their lives to Christ. I believe it is so important to have your kids observing you making decisions with Kingdom priorities.

Throughout my career, I've had lots of chances to share my faith with employees, subcontractors, and clients. One memorable time, a subcontractor told me he accepted the Lord after our conversations. Another time, my bookkeeper Mary, who was into New Age beliefs, called me while I was out of town with a business question and then asked something spiritual. As I shared my views, she started spontaneously praying and accepted Christ right there on the phone. I thought, "Okay, Holy Spirit, I'll step back and get out of the way of what you are doing here." It was amazing to see how the Holy Spirit brought Mary to a real relationship with Jesus.

And then to get to see the impact on her life as she grew in her faith. She truly was transformed!

These experiences showed me how important it is to be open about my faith. God can use anyone, anywhere, to make an eternal difference. It's not about being a Bible-thumper; it's about sharing your authentic life and letting your faith come through naturally in conversations. Christians today often worry about offending people, but by keeping quiet, we miss out on being used by the Holy Spirit to transform lives. We need to be willing to talk about our faith, whether at work, on the soccer field, or wherever. It's those everyday interactions that really make a difference and can have an eternal impact.

So, looking back, I'm grateful for the foundation my parents laid and the path God has guided me on. My kids are continuing that legacy of faith and service. As I move forward, I'm committed to seeing where God is at work and joining Him, whether it's in my job or everyday life. My journey is a testament to the power of saying "yes" to Jesus and letting faith shape every part of life.

PART TWO

Building A Life Of Service

CHAPTER FOUR

DIGGING DITCHES

"Whatever your hands find to do, do it with all your strength." — Ecclesiastes 9:10 (NIV)

It was well-known that Saturdays were workdays around our house. Saturdays meant teamwork and shared responsibility. We knew not to make any plans, because we would be spending the day doing different projects together. Sometimes this looked like changing the oil in the car or working in the yard. Dad used those times to teach us about the value of hard work and how it's just a part of life. I grew up with a solid work ethic, thanks to him.

Around 13, something clicked for me. My dad, being an architect, often took us to construction sites and had us kids help with remodeling projects on our house. And man, I was hooked. I remember thinking, "I know what I want to do when I grow up." That was it for me. I was dead set on becoming a building contractor. Looking back, I now believe God put that desire in my heart and mind.

The high school I went to doubled as a vocational training school, and we had the opportunity to actually build a house from the ground up. We would work from 7 a.m. to 11:30 a.m. every day building this house. We did everything from hand digging the footings to framing, electrical, plumbing, and drywall as well as finish and trim work. It was hard work, but I learned so much from that experience.

Once I graduated, I landed my first real job in construction—digging ditches. This was certainly not a glamorous or high-ranking position, but it was what God had given me. I thought, "Okay, digging ditches is not what I want to do the rest of my life, but as long as I'm a ditch digger, I'm going to be the best ditch digger there is. My ditches are going to be straighter than anyone else's, and they're going to be exactly the right depth." I viewed my work as a ditch digger as me working for the Lord. I wanted to give God my best. Just as it says in Colossians 3:23 (NIV), "And whatever you do, do it heartily, as to the Lord and not to men."

Before long, my boss approached me and offered me an apprenticeship as a carpenter. I jumped at the chance and spent the next two years learning and building my skills. God kept opening doors of opportunity for me, and I kept walking through them in faith.

Right around this time, my family had been hosting a missionary in our home, as they often did. This particular time, we had a Nigerian pastor staying with us. One evening, we got into a conversation about my future plans and where I saw my life going. I thought it was a great plan. I shared my dreams of becoming a building contractor with him, and how I would become very successful, retire at an early age, and then give my time doing missions work abroad. I mean, this sounded like a great plan to me. Even a plan God would like! His response puzzled me initially.

He looked me square in the eyes and paused before speaking. Then, he said to me in his thick Nigerian accent, "Mike, give God the strength of your youth." I was stunned. Hadn't he just heard my fantastic plan? Didn't he understand this plan was even a God-honoring plan (more or less)? This pastor provided a perspective I hadn't really considered before. What would it mean to truly dedicate my youth to God? In the weeks that followed, I replayed those words over and over again in my mind, trying to really understand what he meant. Did God have a plan to use me even as a young person with no real experience, finances, or resources? I slowly started to realize that I needed to hand over my plans and ambitions to God's will completely.

"He is no fool who gives what he cannot keep to gain what he cannot lose." — Jim Elliot

Not long after that conversation, an opportunity popped up at my church. The director of Assisting Indigenous Development (A.I.D.), an organization that approached me, offered me a chance to lead the construction team and train locals in Papua New Guinea. I was nervous, but the pastor's words echoed in my head—"Give God the strength of your youth." The organization's motto was, "Give a man a fish, and you feed him for a day; teach a man to fish, and you feed him for a lifetime." After much prayer and contemplation, I knew what I had to do.

Fortunately, my dad had taught me how to draw design plans when I was in high school, so I understood the design part of what was required. And because of my years of apprenticeship and training, I had enough experience and knowledge to go to Papua New Guinea and build houses there from the ground up, just like I had done in vocational school. Now, I just needed the money to make it happen.

CHAPTER FIVE

OVERCOMING CHALLENGES

"I have told you these things, so that in me you may have peace. In this world you will have trouble. But take heart! I have overcome the world." – John 16:33 (NIV)

Even though I'm not exactly the outgoing type, I knew I had to push past my comfort zone and be obedient. With some encouragement from those around me, I swallowed my pride and reached out to the church. I shared my opportunity and need with them, and within weeks, the congregation had fully funded my trip costs for the entire year's commitment. Something I expected to be a big challenge, raising my support, became something very easy for God. It totally boosted my faith in God's participation in providing!

So, I started packing up the tools I would need and prepared for the trip. I had about 30 pounds of luggage and 70 pounds of tools that I was bringing with me—around 100 pounds total that I would have to carry myself.

When I arrived in Papua New Guinea, one of the first things I realized was that no one really spoke English—except for me. I didn't speak or understand the language there, so I knew immediately that this would create some challenges, and I would soon find out there were a few other things I wasn't totally prepared for.

My first stop on the trip was to a place called Port Moresby, where I would be staying for one night as I traveled to Mount Hagen to meet some of the team. I was given a phone number to call once I arrived so that I could receive instructions on how to get to the hostel where I would be staying, so I began looking for a public phone to use as soon as I landed. And remember, I still had 100 pounds of luggage that I had to drag around with me—and it wasn't the kind of luggage with wheels, either.

I finally got to the phone, and to my surprise, it didn't take US coins. I hadn't realized that all my US currency would need to be exchanged. So, I had to drag all 100 pounds of that luggage back to where I had just come from and get the correct currency.

Eventually, I made it back to the public phone, and this time I was prepared, or so I thought. In the US at that time, if you used a public phone you would make the call first, and then at the end, you would be told how much money you still owed for the call and add more coins to the phone. But this phone was different—and I didn't know it yet.

I put the money in and dialed the number, expecting it to work like it did back home. But each time I said, "Hi, this is Mike," the call would just abruptly end. Turns out, I had to load up the phone with coins first before I could even start talking.

After finally sorting out the phone situation, I hailed a taxi to take me to where I would be staying. The driver didn't speak English, but thankfully I had the address and we managed to get there eventually. Little did I know that was just the beginning of my adventure there.

The next day, I made it back to the airport, caught my flight to Mount Hagen, gathered my luggage, and met my contact, the A.I.D. director, Victor Chamberlin. As I approached what I thought was the passenger side, Victor kindly pointed out that he should probably drive. It dawned on me then—cars drive on the other side of the road here. Talk about a reality check! I felt like a fish out of water, for sure. After a 45-minute ride down a dirt road, we arrived at the compound where the ministry was located.

The very next day, Victor took me out to the worksite, where we were going to build a house for one of the families there. He handed me a sketch on a piece of paper and said, "This is what we'd like to build." I thought, "Okay, there's not a lot of information here, but I think I can work with it." Then he introduced me to the crew. He explained he had to attend to something with the agricultural division that day, so he couldn't stay with me. He emphasized the importance of his task but assured me the guys were more than willing to help out. With that, he drove away, leaving me in the middle of the jungle with eight guys.

I gathered the crew together and asked, "Do any of you speak English?" Nobody raised their hand. I tried again, "English?" No response. So, we resorted to a lot of pointing and gesturing to communicate in what I later learned was Papua New Guinea Pidgin (Tok Pisin). After six weeks of being there and immersed in this new language, I was completely fluent. I really believe that it was a miracle that I could pick up the language in such a short time. Even today, I still remember it. I remember one time I was with another expat who was from Australia who had been working in Papua New Guinea for more than two years and heard me speaking with the locals in Tok Pisin and asked me how long I had been in the country. I told him six weeks. He was totally blown away that I was so fluent. He said that even after two years, he still struggled to communicate with the locals. At that point, I recognized that me plus God equals anything is possible!

Because God had given me the ability to communicate with the team, I was able to start a weekly Bible study with all the guys I worked with. They had very little exposure to the Gospel, so the questions they asked were authentic and raw. I grew up in a Christian-based culture, so I had assumed they would have the same baseline understanding of Christianity that I did, but I quickly realized they did not. These guys had no understanding of the Gospel. They would ask questions like, "Why would Jesus come at all? He's in heaven with all these wonderful things—why would he even care?" I thought to myself, "That's a great place to start."

One guy specifically asked me, "Why did God bring the Gospel to the rest of the world and leave Papua New Guinea out?" He said he felt like they had been left behind, like pigs and dogs running around in the jungle, while the rest of the world got the Gospel. I explained that, unfortunately, their ancestors, like everyone else at the Tower of Babel, had the truth, but they lost it as they dispersed. Now God is giving them the opportunity to hear the Gospel, something their ancestors missed out on. It was eye-opening to hear their perspective. It was both fun and rewarding to help these men grow in their understanding of Scripture and how it applied to their lives.

On one occasion, I was driving from a very remote location to an even more remote location. We were a good distance from Mount Hagen, but this was even farther into the rainforest. The roads were horrible, and the journey to get there was very slow. It was about a 45-minute four-wheeler drive through the rainforest. As I was heading out there, I came across an area with a sloping, open field where land had been cleared and was kind of grassy. There were these two lines of tribes, one on one side, one on the other in that clearing. As I came around the corner, I saw them throwing spears at each other. They were having a tribal war, or at least that's what it looked like to me. I thought, "What are these guys doing? They're throwing spears at each other!"

As I came around the bend and saw this, they all stopped and turned to look at me. Then, they started waving at me as I drove by, and afterward, they went back to throwing their spears at each other. Later, I ran into an anthropologist and told him about the experience. He explained that, often, their tribal warfare is more like sport and entertainment. He also mentioned that their spears don't fly straight because they're made from bent branches and other materials, as straight wood is scarce in the rainforest. The anthropologist said that if the people of Papua New Guinea had invented a straight spear and arrow, like the American Indians, they might have wiped themselves out by now. However, because the spears are bent, they veer off when thrown. I laughed to myself as I drove through, thinking, "I can't believe I'm watching people throw spears at each other."

Reflecting on the man from the tribe I mentioned earlier, he felt as though they had been left out of hearing the Gospel. One interesting thing I learned while I was there was that their society is based on retribution. There was constant warring and fighting in the rainforest between different tribal groups. Almost the entire time I was there, this kind of conflict was always in the background. It often starts with something small, like, "You took my chicken, so I'm going to take your pig. You took my pig, so I'm going to take your daughter. You took my daughter, so I'm going to kill your son. You killed my son, so I'm going to kill your wife." The cycle just keeps escalating back and forth. That's how they interact with each other—there's always tension, always some form of retribution that must be made.

When I was talking with these men during the Bible studies, they would discuss this issue. I would ask, "Why does it keep escalating?" One of the answers was that they had to please and honor their ancestors. They believed their ancestors were watching them, and if they weren't doing what the ancestors wanted, they would get sick, they might die, or they would have other problems. They had witch doctors who would channel what the ancestors wanted or needed. Between trying to please their ancestors and the retribution model of their society, there was always this horrible tension and fighting.

A lot of times, you hear ideas suggesting that we should just leave native peoples alone—that they're peaceful and simply want to live in their own way. However, the men I was speaking to said, "No, we want the Gospel. We want to know a better way to live, we want to improve our society, we don't want to live like this." They saw bringing the Gospel to Papua New Guinea as a huge gift, helping them adopt a new way of thinking, a new way of structuring their society, and a new way of interacting with each other. It was truly eye-opening for me to see how the Gospel appealed to people who had no prior exposure to it, and how they viewed it as something very positive and beneficial to their society.

Looking back on my experiences, I've really started to see how the role of American missionaries in global missions is changing. Nowadays, the focus is more on helping local leaders by giving them the tools and training they need. Organizations like Multiplication Network Ministries do this really well. Back in the day, American and European missionaries were at the forefront when it came to missions, but things have shifted. Now, we're more of a support crew. We're starting to recognize that it's crucial to empower local leaders for long-lasting change.

Even though there's talk about traditional missionary work being outdated and expensive, I still believe American Christians have a huge role to play in global missions. By giving our support—whether through resources, training, or just some words of encouragement—we can really make a difference in spreading God's love.

PART THREE

Global Impact

CHAPTER SIX

FROM COSTA RICA TO KENYA

**"If serving is beneath you, then leadership is
beyond you." – Tim Elmore**

After my initial one-year commitment in Papua New Guinea, the director, Victor, asked if I would consider signing up for an additional year of service. I had been away from my friends and family, missed holidays and birthdays, and gained a whole new appreciation for those who served abroad, separated from their families for long periods. I was conflicted because I wanted to pursue my dream of becoming a building contractor, and yet this was a great opportunity as well. What was I to do? I wasn't sure, so I talked with my dad and my pastor. My dad said, "You gotta listen to God and do whatever He is asking." My pastor said, "Working in the construction business in the United States is a mission field just as much as being in Papua New Guinea." That changed my paradigm, and I began to see the construction industry in a whole new way—as a mission field. After a lot of prayer, I decided to stay in the U.S. and pursue my construction career.

I started out again as a carpenter, determined to work "as unto the Lord" and be the best carpenter I could be. My framing would be straighter, perfectly plumb, and true. After some time, my diligence was recognized, and I worked my way up to project superintendent and then project manager. By 1997, I was buying the business from my father-in-law. We expanded the business, working across states and even overseas, focusing on building specialized facilities for the military and defense sectors.

Cathy and I got married in 1984 and started our family in the late '80s. It was during this period that my church, Skyline Wesleyan—where I had been going since I was born—planned a trip to Costa Rica to help build a church. Something about that project really spoke to me, and after Cathy and I prayed about it, we both felt that God was giving a "yes" to move forward.

Money was tight back then. With a young family and the usual bills, finding an extra $1,200 for the trip seemed nearly impossible. Cathy and I were sticklers for our budget. Many times, at the end of the week, I'd tell her, "You've got $15 for groceries," and she'd figure out a way to make it work. But I knew I had to get creative to participate in this trip and get myself to Costa Rica.

So, I started reaching out to friends with letters, explaining the trip and asking if they'd like to chip in. Thanks to their generosity, I managed to scrape together enough for the trip. It ended up being a group of about eight or nine of us heading over there. We all packed up our clothes and tools and flew from San Diego to San José, Costa Rica. After collecting our bags, we walked outside the airport to a crowded area where we met Pastor Robert and some of the people from his church, who were there to take us to the church. We rode in an old Toyota van that seemed to be at the end of its useful life. Pastor Robert Brantas is a powerhouse in church planting across Central America, with over 135 church plants he has been involved with. It was so encouraging to meet someone with such a passion for expanding God's Kingdom and seeing lives transformed.

As I sat in the back of the old van, driving through downtown San José, I distinctly remember hearing the Holy Spirit say to me, "Mike, I have much for you to do in Costa Rica." I thought, "But Lord, I don't know anything about Costa Rica, I don't speak Spanish, I don't..." I caught myself and thought, "Why am I starting with all the reasons why I can't?" In my spirit, I prayed, "Lord, I am sorry I immediately go to the reason why I can't. I will start with yes until you clearly tell me no." What a grand adventure God had planned for me. Today, as I look back on that moment in the back of the van, I am grateful for the change to "Yes, God." Cathy and I count Pastor Robert and his wife, Anna, as two of our dearest friends. I have experienced miracles and God's presence in ways I am so grateful for. It started with a humble, unsure, tentative "Yes, God."

Pastor Robert's church was small, a humble place with a rough concrete floor and cows peeking in during services because one side of the building was open. We were there to help build a fellowship hall next to the church—a place for cooking and events. We bunked up in Sunday school rooms on makeshift beds during our stay. Despite the language barrier—my Spanish was non-existent, and Pastor Robert spoke primarily Spanish—I could see his deep love for people and his faith. It was truly special.

Back home after that trip, I felt a strong pull to do more in Costa Rica, but I was strapped for resources and time as a business owner with a young family and various ministry commitments. Still, my church went to Costa Rica every year, and I made sure I was on those trips. Determined to bridge the language gap, I started hammering away at Spanish with Rosetta Stone and tapes in my car. Over time, my Spanish got better, and so did Pastor Robert's English. We grew to be good friends and bonded over our shared passion for ministry, especially towards the indigenous people of Central America.

Over the years, we worked with various tribes in the Costa Rican rainforests. Even after I moved on from Skyline, I kept organizing teams to support Pastor Robert's church planting efforts. He always had us help out other churches or indigenous groups instead of just focusing on his own needs, which really impressed me. Saying "yes" to that first trip led to many more—24, in fact, each stamped in my passport, each with its own story.

On one of our early trips, while we were finishing up some drywall, I fell off a makeshift scaffold and knocked myself out cold. The women from the church were in the sanctuary for a prayer meeting. When they heard about my fall, they immediately came over and prayed for me. These ladies were not praying quiet, calm prayers for me; they were praying with passion, very loudly and all at the same time! When I came to, I looked up and saw the circle of ladies around me shouting and praying. I was confused as to what was happening. Then it came to me: I must have fallen and gotten knocked out. As my awareness of what happened started to clarify, I realized I could not move my arms or legs. I thought I was paralyzed, and I was starting to panic, but then I felt this rush of energy shoot through my body, and I could move again—a real-life miracle. Though I still deal with neck pain from that fall, it's a constant reminder of God's protection and grace, much like the apostle Paul's thorn in his flesh. Even though the pain sticks around, it reminds me of God's grace and the miracle of that moment.

After deciding not to return to Papua New Guinea, I focused on my construction career in Southern California. Cathy and I got married two and a half years after I came back from Papua New Guinea.

A few months into our marriage, I received a call from the Lions Training Association, an Australia-based ministry. While working in Papua New Guinea, I got to know several people from this organization since their headquarters were nearby. They called to offer me a position as the director of a new sawmill project in the rainforest. They believed I would be a great fit for the role.

I asked about the current state of the project, and they informed me that there was nothing there yet. They planned to put a sawmill on a truck, send it into the jungle, set it up, train locals to run it, and establish a new training center.

Initially, I considered the offer and discussed it with Cathy. We prayed and thought it through. One of the reasons I had decided to stay in the U.S. and not return to Papua New Guinea was my vision of the construction industry as a mission field. I had developed a passion for this and saw it as a place to minister.

As we evaluated the new opportunity to return to Papua New Guinea, these thoughts kept resurfacing. What about the mission field in the construction industry here? What about the excitement and vision God had placed in my heart? Eventually, we concluded that God was not leading us to take this new opportunity. We felt called to stay in Southern California and minister in the construction industry. The earlier "yes" won out over the new opportunity.

This experience taught us that starting with a "yes" doesn't always mean following through with every opportunity. Sometimes, God provides clarity, and you may end up with a definitive "no." It's important to discern whether a new opportunity is a distraction from God's original vision for you.

One of the funnier memories I have from this time (though it didn't feel funny at the moment) was living in a small one-bedroom house that was a mix of native materials and conventional construction. The house had a wood frame with metal tin on the walls and roof, and the interior walls were made of woven bamboo.

At night, I would often hear noises. I kept a flashlight next to my bed, and when I heard the noises, I would shine it on the walls to see rats crawling around. The noise drove me crazy because it disturbed my sleep. I didn't mind the rats running around, but I needed a good night's sleep. So, I came up with a solution: I placed my shoes—tennis shoes, boots, and flip-flops—next to my bed. When I heard the rats at night, I would grab a shoe and throw it at the wall where the noise was coming from. The rats would scurry off, and I would get some peace for a little while. They were definitely there to stay, so I had to improvise just to get a good night's sleep.

CHAPTER SEVEN

A PASTOR AND A HORSE

Pastor Mario wasn't your typical pastor; he worked in indigenous areas where church is more about mingling with the community than sitting in a pew. He'd roam around visiting different tribal groups, usually gathering under a simple thatch roof supported by poles—really, just the great outdoors turned into a meeting spot.

One time, Pastor Robert and I had some funds to spare, and we thought we'd see what we could do to help out local pastors like Mario. We found out Mario had a pretty tough start; he lost an arm due to a snakebite when he was younger. But while recovering in the hospital, some Christian nurses shared the Gospel with him, and that changed everything. He decided to become a pastor and started ministering to his own people, the Cabecar Indians.

Mario's living situation was pretty rustic and basic—a home made from poles and tin with blankets for walls. He told us about a local rule that was holding him back: you can't build anything permanent until you've paid off your land. With Pastor Robert interpreting, I asked how much he owed on the land. He said, "Oh, it is so much money I can't even tell you." I pressed him to tell us. He finally relented and gave us the amount. Turns out, he only owed $400 on his property. That amount, to Pastor Mario, was something he never imagined he would overcome in his lifetime. So, we sorted that out for him. Then we learned his horse, which he used to visit the village areas throughout the rainforest, had been attacked and killed by a puma. Replacing it would cost $750, another amount that was unattainable for Pastor Mario, which we also managed to handle.

I joked with my wife that night, saying, "Guess what, babe? I just bought property and a horse in Costa Rica." Her response was priceless: "Did we need property and a horse in Costa Rica?" I told her it wasn't for us, but it was still pretty cool. One thing I have learned in my involvement with missions work around the world is that what we Americans consider a little money can make a significant difference for someone serving the Lord in another part of the world. I believe God loves connecting His children who have resources to those in other parts of the world who have a need. It is a blessing for the giver and the one who receives.

We went back to the U.S., raised more funds, and put together a team. When we returned, we built Mario a nice three-bedroom house using a prefab concrete system that was perfect for the setting. Our team and Pastor Robert's people worked side by side on this, even though we didn't all speak the same language. It was amazing to see everyone come together like that.

The project even got some media attention from a national Costa Rican television station, which was great publicity for Pastor Robert's church and their efforts. After we wrapped up, I went back for the handover ceremony, which the local news covered. Seeing Mario and his family get their new home was a real highlight.

Looking back, I'm reminded that living according to God's will doesn't always mean receiving material blessings, but it sure feels like part of it sometimes. My main goal has always been to put God's Kingdom first, and it seems that everything else just falls into place after that. I've been blessed in many ways, financially included, and I credit that to being obedient and faithful to the opportunities and needs God has placed before me.

CHAPTER EIGHT

I SOLD MY PORSCHE

"I believe the only reason God blesses us is so that we can bless others." – Michael J. Gaetke

Ever since high school, my dream car was a Porsche 911. Fast forward 20 years, and I finally got one. It was used, not exactly in pristine condition, but it was mine, and I loved tinkering with it. I had that car for a good ten years, fixing it up and making it my own.

Then came this project in Costa Rica. We were building a house and needed to raise over $30,000. At some point, it just hit me—sell the Porsche. Use that money for the house. Cathy and I talked it over and decided to go for it. Selling that car pushed us past our fundraising goal. And you know what? I've never regretted that decision.

The cool part? A number of years later, God opened a door for me to get another Porsche. It's funny how life works—my dad was always a car guy, and I grew up working on cars with him, just loving the process. And here I was, given another chance to enjoy what I love. Even though I gave up that first Porsche, I was blessed enough to get another shot at owning my dream car.

John Maxwell used to say, "You can't outgive God," and I have found that to be true over and over again!

CHAPTER NINE

THE BIRTH OF AFRICA SERVANT LEADER

"Do all the good you can,
By all the means you can,
In all the ways you can,
In all the places you can,
At all the times you can,
To all the people you can,
As long as ever you can."

— **John Wesley**

I'll be honest with you: Africa was never on my radar. I was perfectly content with my mission work in Latin America and Brazil. But then, I got involved with the Fellowship of Companies for Christ International (FCCI), which helps business folks see their work as a platform for ministry. That's where I met Peter Mulinge from Kenya. Little did I know, this meeting would change everything.

Now, let me back up a bit. Years before we started Africa Servant

Leader, my wife Cathy and I were part of Skyline Church, where John Maxwell was our pastor for 15 years. Many years after John and everyone else had left Skyline, we attended a servant leader conference in San Diego, hosted by Art Barter and the Servant Leadership Institute. John Maxwell was the keynote speaker and, by this time, he was a renowned author and speaker.

At the conference, John was in the back signing books. We had not seen him for more than 10 years. Cathy and I stood nearby, and when John noticed us, he dropped everything and came over to give us big bear hugs. It was like seeing an old friend. He invited us to catch up after he finished signing. We introduced him to Peter Mulinge, who was also there. We shared what we were doing in Kenya with Africa Servant Leader and the amazing things God was doing. Peter was over the moon to get his picture taken with John.

A few years later, Peter was back in Kenya at a leadership event connected to John's organization. He told them he had met John Maxwell, and they were amazed since very few leaders there had actually met him. Peter showed them the pictures, and it was a big deal for everyone. This connection led to a partnership between Africa Servant Leader and John Maxwell's organization, Equip, in Kenya. It's one of those "small world" stories where God orchestrates meetings in incredible ways. A simple encounter in San Diego connected two organizations now working together in Kenya to develop servant leaders.

So, back to Peter. He was in San Diego working on his doctorate in leadership when a mutual friend introduced us, suggesting Peter share his work with our group. Peter's idea was to bring servant leadership to Kenya and the African continent, a concept not widely developed there. He casually mentioned that anyone interested in visiting Kenya was welcome to join him.

I didn't think much of it at first, but then I felt a nudge. I talked it over with Cathy, and although Africa had never been a focus for me, I felt maybe God had a purpose in connecting me with Peter. So, I called Peter and agreed to go with him.

Our trip to Kenya was eye-opening. We taught a three-day seminar on servant leadership to the governor of Makueni County and his executive staff. The governor was impressed, seeing the value of this teaching for Kenya. They don't separate church and state in Kenya like we do, so we could openly pray and sing Christian songs during government meetings.

The governor was so enthusiastic that he wanted us to teach the entire county staff, around 3,000 people. Realizing the scale of the task, we founded a nonprofit, Africa Servant Leadership Development Initiative, to support this work. Since then, the organization has grown, and I remain on the board.

Reflecting on this journey, it's remarkable how far I've come. As a kid, I never imagined traveling the world for ministry. Yet, here I am, looking back at what the Lord has done, and it's truly humbling.

Now, let's talk about the Servant Leader Model. John Maxwell taught me an important lesson: "If you want to be successful, invest in the success of the people around you." As a young business owner, I took this to heart, meeting with employees to understand their vision of success and helping them create a plan to achieve it. This approach was vastly different from most of my peers, who focused primarily on revenue and profit goals. For me, investing in people was paramount. I believed that if we focused on developing people and doing excellent work as if for the Lord, the profits would follow naturally.

Running my construction company using the servant leader model has been central to my approach, both in business and beyond. My main focus as the owner has always been on developing people and giving them opportunities to succeed. It's about investing in others to help them grow, which in turn helps you and your business succeed.

The Servant Leadership Institute, in Carlsbad, CA, established by Art Barter, is all about empowering leaders to serve others as the foundation of their leadership practice. It moves away from traditional hierarchical models, emphasizing that a leader's primary role is to support and develop their team. Key principles of the Servant Leadership Institute include:

- **Prioritizing People:** The core idea is to make people the top priority. Servant leaders ask, "How will I help people?" rather than just, "Will I help people?" This commitment to the growth and success of team members fosters an environment where everyone feels valued and supported.

- **Being Fully Present:** Servant leaders are fully attentive during interactions with their team, setting aside distractions and showing genuine interest in their employees' well-being and professional development. The leader's intent aligns with their actions, demonstrating authenticity and care.

- **Providing and Caring:** It's essential to meet the team's needs, both professionally and personally. This principle became particularly vital during the pandemic, where leaders prioritized the safety and well-being of their employees, creating a supportive environment where they felt secure and appreciated.

- **Recognizing and Rewarding:** Celebrating achievements and recognizing efforts are crucial aspects of servant leadership. By acknowledging and rewarding contributions, leaders motivate their teams and foster a positive, productive work culture, as well as your people feeling a sense of ownership in the business or the mission.

- **Aligning with Core Values:** Servant leadership is deeply rooted in values like integrity, honesty, and excellence. Leaders must ensure their actions are consistent with these values, building trust and respect within the team. This alignment creates a culture of mutual respect and commitment, driving long-term success.

The goal of the Servant Leadership Institute is to transform traditional leadership paradigms by embedding these principles into organizational culture. This leads to more engaged, productive, and loyal teams, benefiting both employees and the organization as a whole. By prioritizing people and fostering an environment of trust and support, servant leadership significantly contributes to sustainable success and profitability.

When you lead as a servant, your employees are happier and more invested in their work. They feel like part of a family, making them want to stick around longer. There are many benefits to using this model that people often overlook. I once read an article discussing how companies using the servant leader model are more profitable due to lower turnover and higher productivity among employees. These hidden advantages make a business not just a better place to work, but also more successful in the long run.

There are several great books written about servant leadership by authors such as Art Barter, Ken Blanchard, John Maxwell, Robert Greenleaf, and others. I would highly encourage you to invest in learning the principles, values, and habits of servant leadership!

Many employees have told me that working at my company was the best employment experience they ever had. That is the highest praise for me as an employer. By prioritizing people, we created a successful business that grew and positively impacted lives. Half of our employees were believers, and the others witnessed the principles of integrity, honesty, and excellence in action. Many came to Christ through their time at our company, simply by observing and interacting with believers in a professional setting. Living out Christian values in business serves as a powerful testimony and can lead to significant transformations in people's lives.

Even when business consultants urged me to set revenue and profit goals, I prioritized goals related to developing people and achieving excellence in service. I believed that focusing on these aspects would naturally lead to financial success. This approach proved successful, both in business growth and in fostering a positive work environment. The result was a thriving business that grew across multiple states and internationally, specializing in the design and construction of military and defense projects. More importantly, it was a place where employees felt valued and supported, leading to lasting positive relationships and spiritual growth for many.

I'm grateful for the influence of mentors like John Maxwell and the foundation of faith and service my parents instilled in me. By focusing on investing in people and living out my faith in the workplace, I've seen firsthand how it can lead to both business success and life transformation. It's a testament to the power of saying "yes" to Jesus and letting faith guide every part of your life.

Expansion in Africa: Kenya, Uganda, and Beyond

Recently, I was able to travel back to Kenya for a significant graduation event with 221 students from nine different counties. There was also a visiting bishop from Uganda, which has paved the way for expanding our efforts into Uganda and Tanzania, with South Africa also on our radar. This expansion aligns perfectly with the original vision Peter had, making it an exciting time to witness God's work in Africa.

Before the graduation, we met with the deputy governor, who attended the ceremony and was so impressed that she signed up for the next class, along with two of her staff members, the very next day. This involvement from government officials is promising. The previous administration in Makueni County was very supportive, with the former governor and his staff participating in the training. Although we haven't yet connected with the new governor, the deputy governor's engagement is a positive step, and we hope to continue our government training initiatives.

I also had the chance to sit down with Peter, the founder, and interview him about his remarkable journey. He came to the U.S. without money or a place to stay, yet God provided for his tuition and living arrangements. Initially, he planned to return home after earning his degree, but opportunities for further education kept presenting themselves. He completed a Master of Divinity and then a Doctorate, all through God's provision and the support of relationships formed along the way. Many of those supporters are still with him today.

From the early days when I was there teaching small classes with Peter, who was then the sole instructor besides myself as a guest, the organization has grown tremendously. Now, there are 24 trained instructors working across the country, and Peter has transitioned into a more presidential role, still teaching trainers but focusing on broader leadership. The organization continues to grow, and God's blessings are evident in the progress we see.

Overall, it's a thrilling time to be involved and witness the incredible things God is doing in Africa.

CHAPTER TEN

CHURCH PLANTING - MULTIPLICATION NETWORK

"You are the only person on earth who can use your ability."– Zig Zigler

The weekly business group I lead through Fellowship of Companies for Christ International (FCCI) led me to connect with Jon Voget, an advancement director for Multiplication Network (MN). He started attending our weekly meetings and mentioned that John Wagenveld, the founder, would be in town occasionally. I said, "Sure, he's welcome to join us and share about his organization."

John would come to the meetings, but he never really talked about MN. Instead, he'd pose some great theological questions or share scripture, sparking amazing conversations. Afterward, we'd grab coffee, and he'd tell me more about his work. Cathy and I even attended a Kingdom Investor Retreat in Palm Springs, learning more about MN, and eventually, we started supporting them. John later asked me to consider joining the board, which, after some prayer,

Cathy and I felt that God was providing a "Yes," and we agreed it was the right move.

Cathy and I really connected with the group. The organization's focus is on planting churches, and last year, with their ministry partners, they planted over 11,000 churches in more than 60 countries. It's incredible to see what God is doing through them. During one of the retreats, John suggested that with our newfound free time after selling the company, we might consider incorporating ministry into our extended travels.

Cathy and I had been doing marriage ministry at our church, using curriculums like Love and Respect and The Five Love Languages. We thought, why not take this on the road? John loved the idea and suggested we start with the Latin America hub in Ecuador. He mentioned about 10 couples who could benefit from such a retreat.

We prayed about it and felt God was giving us a "yes." We bought all the materials in Spanish and had the couples complete assessments through the Prepare and Enrich program. Cathy, being a licensed Marriage and Family Therapist, handled this perfectly. We took all the materials with us to Ecuador and held a weekend marriage retreat with the leadership there.

Even though we had hoped to stay for a month, we were only there for about a week. The weekend conference was powerful. We had an amazing translator, and the Holy Spirit was definitely present. The participants were so open about their marriages, sharing struggles like anger issues and seeking help. We provided tools and counseling resources, and we could see God working in their lives.

This experience was a huge blessing. Cathy has always been supportive of the ministries I've been involved in, even when it meant she would join me trekking through the rainforest in Costa Rica. It was special to do something that was on both of our hearts together. There's nothing greater than experiencing God's work alongside your spouse. When I first met John, I never imagined it would lead to Cathy and me leading a marriage retreat in Quito, Ecuador. It's amazing how God weaves these opportunities into our lives.

More recently, in 2022, Cathy and I attended a Multiplication Network conference in Mexico City. We gathered 28 different denominations and over 250 church pastors and leaders. Each denomination took turns sharing their insights and lessons learned about church planting. For instance, the Assemblies of God would present their best practices from the past year, followed by the Foursquare Church, who would lay hands on their leaders, pray for them, and then share their own experiences.

What really stood out to me was seeing all these denominations, despite their differences, come together in prayer. It was powerful and moving. Where else do you witness such unity in the body of Christ? Denominations putting aside their differences to focus on what unites them—prayer and shared goals.

Had I not said "yes" to getting involved with this organization, I would have missed out on witnessing something truly extraordinary. It was a real move of God, seeing these denominations come together through their commitment to church planting. United by this common goal, it was inspiring to be a part of it.

PART FOUR

Everyday Ministry

CHAPTER ELEVEN

MY FIRST DAY IN PRISON

**"When I am surrounded by God's activity and God opens
my eyes to recognize His work, I always assume He
wants me to join Him." – Henry Blackaby**

I was at the Metropolitan Correctional Center in downtown
San Diego with Steve, getting ready to start a Bible study
on the 10th floor, when we met JJ. Behind those heavy steel bars,
he threw us a curveball right off the bat: "I don't believe in God; I
believe in Satan. I worship Satan," he declared. That was my first real
taste of the conversations I'd be having with inmates.

JJ was all in on his belief that Satan had the upper hand,
completely dismissing any idea of God's power. Covered in gang
tattoos and with a steely gaze, he definitely looked the part. After
he finished, I was standing there and felt this intense jolt, like a
surge of electricity through my body. I stepped toward him, looked
him in the eye, and said, "JJ, you're being deceived. Satan's feeding
you lies from the depths of hell. But you know what? Jesus Christ

beats Satan every single time. Jesus has the real power. He's about forgiveness, peace, and a chance to start fresh." I could feel the Holy Spirit empowering me with the words as they came.

JJ was visibly shaken as I spoke. Sweat started beading on his forehead, and he muttered, "Your words are hitting me hard." "That's the Holy Spirit at work," I told him. I asked JJ to join us for the Bible study that was about to start, and although he wasn't ready to join us just yet, he didn't mind if we prayed for him.

So, we prayed right there, and I watched something amazing happen. JJ's initial defiance softened into something more open, more willing. It was an incredible moment to witness, and it marked just the beginning of my path into prison ministry.

This whole journey started when my neighbor Steve introduced me to Prison Fellowship, a program for inmates. Again, another opportunity God was placing in front of me. My prayer was, "Okay, God, let me start with a "yes" attitude and see if You provide any reasons why I should not go forward." You guessed it—Cathy and I prayed about it and felt the answer was "yes," so I went through all the necessary training and clearance to become an in-prison volunteer.

When Steve and I met outside the prison that first day, we went through the usual security checks and passed through those imposing steel doors—they closed with a loud KA-BAM. Inside, it was a different world—noisy, bustling, and filled with the sharp scents of cleaners and laundry.

We managed to pull together a group of inmates interested in our Bible study. It was a genuine, raw session where each man shared his story and thoughts on the scriptures we read.

After the session, we made our way out, leaving the echoes of the prison behind us as the San Diego skyline reminded us of the outside world. Driving home, I felt a profound sense of gratitude and purpose. I knew the Holy Spirit was moving not just in those men, but in me too. Reflecting on the day, I promised myself—and God—that I wouldn't take my freedom for granted, not just the physical kind, but the spiritual freedom I had too.

About three or four years later, I was at the prison sharing that story with a bunch of guys. We were sitting around a table, probably a dozen of us. Frank, the guy next to me, was listening intently as I talked about JJ. I wrapped up the story by saying, "I don't know what happened to JJ. He never came back, and I haven't seen him since, but I still pray for him whenever God brings him to my mind."

Then Frank turned to me and said, "Can I be a JJ for you?" I was a bit puzzled and asked, "What do you mean, Frank?" He explained, "Can you remember me years from now and pray for me?" I said, "Absolutely, Frank. Whenever God brings you to my mind, I'll pray for you."

Next to Frank was a guy named Javier, who chimed in, "Can you remember me too?" Then a guy named Jose asked the same. It went around the table, each one wanting to be remembered and prayed for because they didn't have anyone else in their lives doing that for them. I've got this mental list now, and I still pray for those guys whenever they come to mind, which they often do.

One day, years later, I was walking into a grocery store when a guy stopped me. "Mike?" he asked. I recognized him but couldn't place where I knew him from. He said, "Mike, it's Alan. I was in prison, and you were there for the Bible studies." Suddenly, it clicked. I asked him how he was doing. He shared how he had accepted Christ while in prison and how I helped him see the truth. He'd been out for about a year, helping others integrate into society when getting out of prison, writing a book, and starting a ministry. Right there, outside the grocery store, we stopped and prayed to praise God and pray for his new ministry. It was such a cool moment, seeing how God had transformed his life.

Another memorable moment happened in prison with a guy named Joshua. He was new to our Bible study, and he introduced himself by saying, "I've got a crazy story. I was a pastor in Los Angeles, saved from a gang life. I prayed to God to give me an opportunity to minister to prisoners, and then I got arrested for past crimes. Here I am, in prison, ready to serve. God answered my prayer, but not quite the way I was expecting!" Over the months, Joshua led Bible studies and brought others to Christ. Being a former gang member, he could really relate to the guys. I helped him with resources, like study Bibles, to support his prison ministry. He made a huge impact while he was there.

Another time, I was asked to cover a Bible study on the 11th floor. Usually, I worked on the 10th floor and didn't know anyone on the 11th. I announced the study, and about 25 guys showed up. Since I was not fluent in Spanish at the time, I asked for a volunteer to interpret. One guy stepped up and said they usually just listened to sermons instead of doing a Bible study, so I switched gears and decided to teach.

God put it on my heart to talk about being adopted as sons of God, having a Heavenly Father who loves them unconditionally. As I spoke, I saw some of the guys starting to cry. The Holy Spirit was moving powerfully. At the end, I invited anyone who wanted to accept Christ to come forward. To my amazement, all 25 of them stood up and joined me. I double-checked through the interpreter to make sure they understood the commitment. They all did, so I led them in a prayer to accept Christ.

Normally, I'd sit down and talk and pray with them one-on-one, but with so many, I had them break into small groups to pray for each other. The Holy Spirit filled the room—people were praying, singing, and speaking in tongues. It was incredible. The guard came over, wondering what was happening. I told him, "The Holy Spirit is at work. These guys have decided to give their lives to God and let Him change their lives."

It was one of those unforgettable moments where you see how God can move powerfully, even in the most unlikely places, with the most unlikely people, including me as a teacher in a prison.

I don't know how much time had passed, but the guard was getting a little anxious, like we needed to wrap this thing up, whatever was happening here. So I kind of got everyone's attention and said, "Let me just pray over you guys. We're going to have to wrap up our time for this meeting." So then I prayed over them and left, thinking, "Okay, I've never experienced anything like that in my life. That was amazing, Lord." When those guys came back the following week, they called me up and said, "I don't know what in the world happened with that group up there." And I said, "I can't explain it. I can tell you what I observed, but it was like revival broke out or something." They responded, "Yeah, we can tell something is really—you know, they're all on fire. They're all just ready to go conquer the world for Jesus." That was nothing of my doing other than saying "yes", again. I could have said, "I only do the 10th floor," but there was the opportunity to go to the 11th floor. I didn't know anybody, but I just wanted to see what God does. And God did some amazing things. So, another opportunity to say "yes", and another crazy, amazing adventure that God put in front of me.

Before I started the in-prison ministry, I had been privileged to lead several people to Christ, but I would say no more than a dozen in my whole life, leading up to that point. I think I was in my mid-40s when I started doing prison ministry, and over the 10 years that I did the in-prison ministry, I would guess that I got to pray with over 700 people to receive Christ. And there is nothing as a believer that is so incredible as to sit with another person and pray with them as they're turning their life over to Christ and accepting Him. And that's a joy, an amazing experience and adventure that, when I talk to a lot of believers, they've often never had the opportunity to experience even once. I can't even imagine missing out on that. But by saying "yes" to God, not only did I get to experience that a few times, but it was literally over 700 times over the 10 years. I just praise the Lord that I had that opportunity. I think about the first conversation I had with my neighbor, who had mentioned, "Yeah, I do prison ministry," and I had mentioned, "Hey, I'd be interested in doing that at some point." And if I hadn't had that conversation and had the opportunity to say "yes", I would have missed out on the incredible joy of being involved in what God was doing at the Federal Prison downtown in San Diego.

CHAPTER TWELVE

LORD, SEND ME!
(TO THE GAS STATION)

"Preach the Gospel at all times. Use words if necessary."
— St. Francis of Assisi

I've made it a point to start each day with a couple of prayers. One is, "Lord, please don't let me overlook the people You place in my path," and the other is, "Lord, what adventure do You have for me today?" I'm usually very task-oriented, always focused on getting things done. My focus can be so sharp on tasks that I might unintentionally ignore people if they're in the way of what I need to accomplish. So, I consciously ask for help to not just step over these folks, because, in the end, material things don't hold eternal value, even though they often dominate our goals.

Working in building design and construction, I'm always wrapped up in projects, from the concept to the actual construction. It's fulfilling, but it can make you sideline people without even realizing it. That's why I've been asking the Holy Spirit to help me remember that people last forever—things don't.

There's one time this really hit home. I was up in Central California for a project, and on my way back, I stopped at an In-N-Out Burger right before hitting the Grapevine. As I sat there eating, I noticed a van parked outside with a sign on the windshield that read, "Need Gas." Initially, I just thought, "Poor guy, should've planned better." But as I ate, I felt this nudge from the Holy Spirit telling me to go talk to them, even though I was anxious to get home and beat the traffic.

I finished up and went over. The guy, Jerry, was there with his wife, Anne. He shared a heartbreaking story about visiting his brother with cancer, possibly for the last time, and now they were trying to get back home. Part of me was skeptical—people can have all sorts of stories—but I felt this push to just go ahead and buy them some gas.

So, we went across to a gas station, I popped my card in, and started filling up their tank. After a good amount had gone in, Jerry, looking relieved, pulled the nozzle out. That's when I took the chance to say, "I'm doing this because I'm a follower of Jesus Christ, and I am buying you this gas in the name of Jesus." A friend had challenged me to give credit to Jesus whenever I helped someone, so that is what I do when I help anyone.

Turns out, Jerry and his wife were praying to the same Jesus I follow, right there on the side of the road, for someone to help them. He told me, "Mike, we're believers too, and we just asked God to send someone." That moment really got to me. Here I was, hesitant and almost ignoring that nudge, but in the end, I was the answer to their prayer. It was a powerful reminder of how a small act of kindness can be a profound response to someone else's needs.

It really showed me the importance of pausing to see the people around you, not just rushing past life's little calls for help. It's about being open to saying "yes" to God in those unplanned moments, which might seem small to us but are huge to someone else.

Many times, we pray, "Lord, send me to the ends of the earth. Send me anywhere, globally." But then, He's like, "I'm sending you down the street. Yeah, to that person in the grocery store you really don't want to talk to." But that's the thing—when you pray that kind of all-encompassing prayer, declaring, "I will go where You want me to go," it really could mean just around the corner, or it could indeed mean Costa Rica or Papua New Guinea.

That heart for missions is about serving God's people everywhere, not just in far-off places. I love how Jesus put it—you know, reaching out to Judea, Samaria, and then to the ends of the earth. It's not about choosing one over the other; it's about embracing them all simultaneously. It's understanding that mission work isn't always about crossing oceans; sometimes, it's about crossing the street. It's about seeing the divine in everyday encounters and being ready to act on it, no matter where we are.

And I think sometimes it can even seem easier to say, "Oh, I'll go across the world." It can be easier to do that than to handle the little things. As we hear in Scripture, "Be faithful with the small, then you'll be given more and more." But to be obedient in the little things means that God can then trust you with the bigger journeys. Yet, for whatever reason, it's sometimes easier to say "yes" to the grand adventures.

That's the scripture I like to refer to when I talk about starting as a ditch digger. Being faithful in the small things, being the best you can be wherever God places you, no matter how insignificant you might perceive it to be. God uses those moments to grow you, to mature you, to help you see a bigger picture of what He wants to accomplish. And then, as you prove trustworthy, He entrusts you with more and more.

It's about not just waiting for the big assignments to prove your faithfulness, but showing it day in and day out in everyday tasks and interactions. This approach not only prepares you for bigger tasks ahead but also deepens your understanding and relationship with God as you learn to see His hand in every part of your life.

CHAPTER THIRTEEN

HOME GROUP AND MINISTRY MEMORIES (FAITH IN ACTION)

"The issue is not prioritizing your schedule, it is scheduling your priorities." – Tim Elmore

Growing up, I never really saw myself as a leader. I always thought of myself more as a follower. But as I started saying "yes" to God in the small things, He began opening doors for me to do more. One of those opportunities came when my wife, Cathy, and I were asked to lead a home fellowship group at our church, Skyline. We were hesitant at first, thinking maybe someone else might be better equipped for this, but we have learned to pray with an attitude of "yes" first. We believed God was providing a "yes" and decided to go for it.

Cathy has this incredible gift for hospitality. She's just naturally outgoing and has a way of making everyone feel truly welcome, seen, and loved. Together, we found that we complemented each other well—I would lead the study, and she would make everyone feel at home.

God really blessed that ministry. Skyline's approach was to grow your group and then raise up an apprentice. When the group got big enough, it would "multiply." The apprentice would take over the original group, and Cathy and I would start a new one with a few other couples. Over the years, we did this multiple times, and it was amazing to see how much growth happened, both in the ministry and in us.

I also got to use my guitar skills to lead worship songs in our groups, which added another layer to our gatherings. Eventually, that led to even bigger roles. Larry Clark, the worship leader from our joint venture Sunday school class, which was quite large, asked me to join the worship team as a guitarist and singer. I said "yes" and played every Sunday in a supporting role.

Then, as our church expanded to another campus, Pastor Dan Reiland, who had a significant impact on my life, asked me to be the worship leader for a new group there. What started as leading worship in a small home group turned into leading a team of musicians and singers for a congregation of hundreds. I ended up doing this for over 20 years across the two campuses, and it was an incredibly rich and fulfilling experience.

Our home was always buzzing with activity, especially on group nights. We'd get the kids ready for bed before everyone arrived, and then start the evening with worship. My kids have told me how special it was to fall asleep to the sounds of our group worship—it wasn't just a blessing for the people in the group, but for our family as well.

All these experiences have taught me the value of saying "yes" in the small things and seeing where God takes them. It's been a journey of growth, not just for me but for everyone around me.

CHAPTER FOURTEEN

THE MOVIE THEATRE

I t's important to me that I don't come off like I always know what I'm doing, always make the right call, or that I am anyone special. So, there was this one time, right after Cathy and I got married, way before we had kids. We used to hit the matinee movies on the weekends—a little tradition of ours.

One Saturday, we ended up sitting next to a young woman with her two-year-old daughter. Her husband was deployed with the Navy. Cathy, using her gift of hospitality, struck up a conversation with her before the movie started. Pretty soon, her little girl was giggling on Cathy's lap as we all swapped stories and had a few laughs. After the movie, we all felt like old friends, saying how great it was to meet each other.

As we were leaving the theater, Cathy turned to me and mentioned we should've asked for her contact info, maybe even invited her over for dinner. She was here all alone with her kid, family miles away in another state, and her husband overseas. I felt the same way—like we should do something. So, we decided to go find her and make the offer. But she was nowhere to be found, not in the lobby or the parking lot. It was as if she had disappeared. We knew only her first name and her daughter's, nothing more. We drove around looking for a bit, but no luck.

We left the parking lot feeling like we missed a clear signal to reach out. That incident really stuck with us. It taught us a tough lesson about following those sudden urges to act, those moments when you feel pushed to do something kind—even if it's out of your comfort zone. If you get that feeling, that nudge from the Holy Spirit, you just gotta go for it and not worry about the what-ifs. We didn't, and we regretted it. None of us are perfect, but hopefully, we learn from these missed chances.

CHAPTER FIFTEEN

THE JH RANCH EXPERIENCE

"You only live once, but if you do it right, once is enough." – Bruce Johnston

One of the most impactful adventures we embarked on as a family was through a connection our kids' school had with a place called JH Ranch in Northern California. JH Ranch offers father-son and father-daughter camps, where you spend a week engaging in high-adventure activities like rope climbing, lake swimming, and whitewater rafting. What sets JH Ranch apart is how they weave spiritual concepts into each activity.

When we first heard about the camp, we thought it was too expensive given our financial situation at the time. But our youngest son, Paul, was in a place where we felt he needed something impactful, and Cathy suggested that maybe JH Ranch would be beneficial for him. After some consideration, we decided to go for it. Paul and I ended up going, and it was an incredible experience. The founder, Bruce Johnston, was the main speaker, and he introduced a model he called "the four seasons" of parenting: Caretaker, Cop, Coach, and Consultant.

Caretaker: When your children are young and need you to care for them.

Cop: During the teenage years, when you're keeping them on the right path and setting boundaries.

Coach: As they grow older and start making more of their own decisions, you guide them like a coach.

Consultant: Once they've moved out and started their own lives, you become a consultant, offering advice when they seek it.

Paul and I had such a positive experience that we decided to take our other kids, Nicole and David, in subsequent summers. Each trip was meaningful and fostered deep connections. Cathy often joked about how I got to do all the fun stuff, but those trips were truly special for me and the kids.

The impact of those experiences is something I have asked my kids about often. Spending one-on-one time with them at JH Ranch communicated value and showed them how much their mom and I cared about our relationship. The teaching moments, spiritual lessons, and shared adventures left lasting impressions on both them and me. Nicole even worked on staff there after graduating from high school and had great adventures of her own.

One of the experiences that stands out in my journey was taking the kids to JH Ranch. It was during my first visit with Paul that I sensed the Holy Spirit wanting to communicate something significant to me. At that time, I was heavily involved in mission work in Costa Rica, and I was eagerly anticipating a revelation or a new focus for our ministry there.

As I prayed and meditated, I kept feeling that there was a message God wanted to give me. I was ready and excited, thinking it would be about our work in Costa Rica. However, what I heard was, "Love your wife." My initial reaction was, "Yes, of course, I love my wife. But what about Costa Rica?" I expected a different message, something more aligned with my mission work. Yet, the message came again: "Love your wife."

Cathy and I had been going through a rough patch before my trip to JH Ranch. Unbeknownst to me, while I was away, Cathy had decided that when I returned, we needed to have a serious conversation about making changes in our relationship. So, when I finally accepted that the message from God was to "Love your wife," I knew I had to take it seriously.

Upon returning home, I told Cathy I had something important to share. She said she had something to tell me too but insisted I go first. I confessed that during my time at the ranch, I had sensed God repeatedly telling me to love her better and to focus on our relationship. Initially, I didn't want to share this because it felt too personal, and I didn't want to be held accountable. But I knew it was important.

To my surprise, Cathy said that my message was exactly what she needed to hear. It was a turning point in our relationship. God had made it clear that I needed to prioritize loving my wife better, and sharing that realization with Cathy marked a new beginning for us. It set a new benchmark from which we could work on and improve our relationship.

Had I not said "yes" to the JH Ranch experience, I might not have received that crucial message. It was a lesson in listening to God, even when His message isn't what you expect, and it ultimately led to a significant improvement in our marriage. Cathy believed this story was important to include, as it highlights the impact of divine guidance on our personal relationships.

PART FIVE

Reflecting on a Life of No Regrets

CHAPTER SIXTEEN

FAMILY AND STEWARDSHIP: BUILDING A LEGACY

"He calls us to trust Him so completely that we are unafraid to put ourselves in situations where we will be in trouble if He doesn't come through." – Francis Chan

One pivotal moment in our family life was when our oldest son, David, was diagnosed with a severe form of AML leukemia just a few months before his fourth birthday. My wife, Cathy, had noticed he was bruising easily and not healing well. The doctor's urgent instructions to get him to the hospital turned our world upside down.

The doctors started him immediately on chemo and other life-sustaining drugs, but David's little body did not respond, even after several rounds of chemotherapy. After three weeks of David receiving treatment in the hospital, our doctor said he needed to meet with Cathy and me. We shuffled into a small conference room to meet with our doctor, and he did not look happy. We knew bad news was on the way. He said, "We have done everything we can for

David. His body has not responded. In fact, his leukemia levels are higher now than when we started, and we are now at a point where all we can do is make him comfortable until he dies." Talk about a blow to the gut. We were devastated.

That happened to be a night I was scheduled to stay with David. We had a cot set up in his room for Cathy or me to stay with him, and he always had one of us with him there at the hospital. Before Cathy left for the night, I said I needed to get some fresh air. I walked out into the parking lot; it was a clear, cool night with a lot of stars. I looked up to the stars and began to pray and cry, "God, I don't understand why you would give us a beautiful son and then take him home so early in his life." As I prayed, I had a vision in my mind of the throne of heaven, grand and glorious, stretching as far as I could see from left to right. On the throne was Jesus looking at me. I began to weep, and in my mind, I was carrying David in my arms. I walked up to Jesus and said, "Lord, we sure would like to keep David, but I know he belongs to you, and I am giving him back to you. I will accept whatever you decide to do with him." As I handed David over to Jesus, he asked me, "What about your other children?" I didn't understand at first, but I realized I needed to give my other two children, Nicole and Paul, to Jesus as well. In my mind, I did the same with Nicole and Paul, giving them back to Jesus. Then Jesus asked me, "What about your wife?" "Yes, Lord, I give Cathy back to you." "What about your business?" "Yes, Lord, the business is yours." "What about your house and possessions?" "Yes, Lord, everything is yours, and I give it back to you." In that moment, I truly came to realize I am only a steward of everything in my life, and God has allowed me to give these things all back to Him. This realization of being a steward of literally everything in my life has had a huge impact on me and changed my life and perspective profoundly.

David's journey through treatment had several memorable moments that reminded us of God's presence. One such moment was when a bird landed on his hospital windowsill, and David joyfully exclaimed, "Look, Mom, God brought a bird to visit me today because my friends can't come." It was a small, beautiful sign of God's care for him.

David went into remission quickly, thanks to an experimental Phase 1 trial drug and, I believe, a supernatural hand. However, the next step in his treatment was an experimental autologous bone marrow transplant, which required us to relocate to Los Angeles temporarily. This procedure involved taking David's own bone marrow, treating it, and then reintroducing it into his body after eliminating the remaining bone marrow.

During this period, Cathy stayed in LA with David during the week, while I remained in San Diego, working and taking care of our other children, Paul and Nicole, with help from our mothers. Every Thursday night, I would drive up to LA with the kids. Cathy would then spend the weekend with Paul and Nicole at an apartment we had rented, while I stayed with David at the hospital. This arrangement made our lives feel like two ships passing in the night, constantly moving but rarely connecting.

One weekend, Cathy's mom joined us, allowing Cathy and me to have dinner together. It was during this rare moment of togetherness that we acknowledged how strained our relationship had become. We realized that we weren't meeting each other's needs and that the stress of our situation was taking a toll on our marriage. However, despite the challenges, we knew we had to push through. We didn't have a clear solution to our problems, but we had faith in God and in each other. We made a pact to keep going, trusting that things would eventually improve.

Reflecting on David's life today—he is 36, married, and has two adopted daughters—fills me with immense gratitude. The support from our church during that time, through meals, prayers, and visits, was invaluable. David's simple faith and joy in small things have inspired me to live each day with trust and optimism, appreciating the beauty around me. This period of intense reliance on the Lord and mutual understanding marked a testament to our faith and dedication to our family. Our commitment to persevere, even in the face of overwhelming odds, ensured that we could eventually focus on rebuilding our relationship and finding a new sense of normalcy.

CHAPTER SEVENTEEN

THE RIGHT PEOPLE
AT THE RIGHT TIME

Early on in running my business, I quickly realized there was a
lot I didn't know. I needed to learn. At the time, I was leading
worship at Skyline Church and was involved in a Sunday class with
Dan Reiland for young married couples called Joint Venture. On the
worship team with me was Ron Kraft, an acoustic guitar player and
vocalist, who also happened to be a business professor at a college in
San Diego.

It's amazing how God places people in your path just when you
need them. One day, Ron and I were chatting, and I mentioned
that I might sign up for one of his classes. He told me he also did
consulting and offered to meet with me once a week to help me
out. Ron wasn't just doing this on the side; he had a full consulting
business. We started meeting weekly, and he guided me through the
basics of business.

As a young business owner, there was so much I didn't know.
Ron taught me how to read financial statements, understand basic
business principles, and conduct SWOT analyses—looking at

strengths, weaknesses, opportunities, and threats. These concepts might seem basic to many businesspeople, but they were game-changers for me. Ron's insights provided new ways to look at and understand my business.

For about three or four years, Ron and I met weekly. During the week, if something came up, I knew I had someone to talk to who could provide valuable input. Whether it was a system that wasn't working right or a strategic decision I needed to make, Ron was there to help me navigate through it. His knowledge and expertise were invaluable. Looking back, I can see that God brought Ron into my life at the perfect time. His guidance was crucial for my business's success. It's clear that this was God's perfect timing, providing exactly what I needed when I needed it. The regular meetings with Ron gave me a sounding board for ideas and a mentor who could guide me through the complexities of running a business.

Ron's influence helped shape my approach to business. His mentoring taught me not just about financials and strategy but also about the importance of investing in people and maintaining integrity in all business dealings. This holistic approach to business, focusing on both people and performance, has been a cornerstone of my career.

CHAPTER EIGHTEEN

A FIVE-YEAR PLAN AT EIGHTY-FIVE

"Your potential is the sum of all the possibilities God has for your life." – Charles Stanley

When I think about longevity in ministry and serving God faithfully, a particular board meeting comes to mind. The founding pastor of Skyline Church, Pastor Orval Butcher, was 85 years old at the time. This was a meeting for the ministry he had founded after "retiring" from being the senior pastor at Skyline, and I was on his ministry board along with Ted Engstrom, who had been the president of World Vision and was then President Emeritus. Ted was probably close to 90 at that time.

We were in a board meeting, and Pastor Butcher was giving his report, talking about his recent activities and the state of the ministry. His tone of voice and the direction of his conversation seemed to hint that he saw his time there winding down due to his age. Ted, being the straightforward guy he was, interrupted him. It was classic Ted. He looked at Orval and said, "Orval, I want to know what your five-year plan is. Where do you see yourself in five years? When you're 90 years old, what are you going to be doing? How are you going to be involved? What are you going to accomplish?"

He was firing off all these questions, and you could see Pastor Butcher looking at him like, "Five-year plan at 85? What am I going to be doing at 90?" It was impressive. Ted was just relentless, always pressing forward. He wasn't about to let anyone off the hook just because they were older. He wasn't saying, "Okay, you're old, you've done a lot, now take it easy."

Maybe I'll feel different when I'm 85, but at the time, it really struck me that Ted wanted Pastor Butcher to have a five-year plan with all these details. At 85! Most people at that age think they've done all they're going to do. But Ted's attitude was all about having a plan, keeping the momentum, and not just coasting. Ted's attitude was, "Saying yes to God is an activity that never expires."

Ted and I had a lot of conversations over the years on the board with Pastor Butcher. He was such a great encouragement—no-nonsense and straight to the point. He spoke a lot of wisdom into my life, especially about missions and reaching people around the world. He always said there's no reason you can't do anything if you believe God can use you, and when God calls you to do something, He will equip you for that call. That really helped me see that it doesn't matter who I am; I'm just a vessel. If I'm a willing vessel, God can use me in ways I never imagined.

Ted's approach made me realize that being proactive and having a plan isn't just for the young. It's about being available and ready for what's next, no matter your age. It's a mindset that keeps you moving forward, always looking for the next opportunity to serve and make a difference.

CHAPTER NINETEEN

MENTORING AT HOME

Because of the incredible mentors I had in my life, I knew I wanted to become that for others down the road. One of the pivotal moments in my journey as a mentor came when Cathy, my wife, pointed out something crucial. She noticed how much time I was investing in mentoring younger Christian business guys, helping them develop their understanding of their purpose and guiding them in being better fathers and men of God. This was during the years when our kids were transitioning from grade school to junior high and high school. One day, Cathy asked me, "What about your own sons? Are you mentoring and teaching them?"

Cathy has an incredible knack for seeing things I might be blind to, and her question hit me hard. Here I was, spending a lot of time mentoring others, but what about my own children? It was a wake-up call that made me realize I needed to be just as intentional about mentoring my own sons and daughter.

"Our greatest fear should not be of failure, but of succeeding in life at things that do not matter." — *Francis Chan*

I began thinking about how to apply the same principles I used with the young men I mentored to my children. I looked into books and resources aimed at adolescents and found that some of the materials I used for mentoring adults had teenage versions. One such book was The *7 Habits of Highly Effective Teens*, based on the transformational book The *7 Habits of Highly Effective People*. I decided to go through it with my sons.

As my kids entered their teenage years, we started a tradition of annual staycations in Mission Beach, San Diego. Before many of these vacations, I would assign a book for everyone in our family to read. This became a family activity where we would have discussions around the book, covering both spiritual and secular topics. One memorable discussion was about the concept of "margin"—having space and balance in your life.

My kids used to joke about having homework assignments during their vacations, but it led to some wonderful, meaningful conversations. They would often remind me about the principles we discussed when I needed to hear them, like when they'd ask, "Dad, do you have enough margin in that area of your life?" It was heartening to see them internalize these lessons and even mentor me in return, keeping me on track with the lessons Cathy and I had taught them.

Cathy and I also made it a point throughout most of our marriage to do a daily devotion together every morning. This time of getting into the Word and discussing spiritual ideas helped us grow together and fostered a strong spiritual foundation in our marriage. It's not a mentoring relationship, but a journey of learning together, which is essential in any marriage. I'm not saying we've done it perfectly, but I sure know when we get off track with time together, we get off track!

"You cannot go back and change the beginning, but you can start where you are and change the ending." — C.S. Lewis

One of the key lessons I've learned and now share with others is that your first ministry is your family. I have seen in my own life that when you get busy with ministry activities, it is too easy to start believing what you are doing is so important that you neglect your first ministry—your family. As the Bible says, "What good is it if a man gains the world, but loses his soul?" We can take that idea to the next logical thought: "What good is it if a man gains the world, but neglects the spiritual health of his family, and they lose their soul?" Whether we are busy with work or ministry, it is so important not to neglect the first ministry of our families!

When your kids are young, it's incredibly easy to get caught up in the busyness of life. With sports, school activities, and social events, the days can quickly become a blur. That's why it's crucial to be proactive and deliberate about spending time with your children. These meaningful moments and lessons aren't just going to happen on their own. If you don't make the effort and commitment to mentor, teach, and raise your own kids, the world will step in and do it for you. And trust me, you want to be the primary influence in their lives.

I'm incredibly thankful to the Lord today. My kids are all in their mid-30s, and we still have a wonderful relationship with each one of them. Each of them is a Christ follower, loves the Lord, and is involved in ministry. The time and effort invested in them have paid tremendous dividends, not just in their lives but also in the lives of others they touch.

CHAPTER TWENTY

JOSHUA'S MEN

"You can't live the Christian life without a band of Christian friends, without a family of believers in which you find a place." – Tim Keller

Back when Cathy and I were newly married, I was asked to participate in a program in the late 1990s that Pastor Dan Reiland developed. Every year, he took about 8 to 12 guys through this program. We'd read books—both secular and religious—one book a month, and then meet one day a month to discuss them. We'd get discussion questions ahead of time, and we'd have various assignments to complete before our meetings.

Some of the books we read came at just the right time in my life. I still remember some of the secular ones, like *Seven Habits of Highly Effective People* by Stephen Covey. Even today, I quote things from that book when mentoring and talking with people. One of my favorite quotes is, "Seek first to understand, then to be understood." I probably use that several times a month because it's so relevant in many situations. Covey's habits, like "sharpening the saw," were incredibly powerful for me as a young business owner and father.

We also read classics like *How to Win Friends and Influence People* by Dale Carnegie and *Celebration of Discipline* by Richard Foster, which provided a great foundation for spiritual growth. Discussing these books with other men who were in the same stage of life, under the guidance of someone as wise as Dan Reiland, was incredibly impactful.

We did more than just read books; we also gave presentations to the group. This helped me gain confidence in speaking and presenting, which was crucial as I was developing my skills in those areas. The feedback and encouragement I received were invaluable.

This program didn't just improve my business acumen and presentation skills—it profoundly influenced every aspect of my life. It made me a better father, husband, business owner, and friend. It helped me mentor other guys and impacted how I approached my faith and relationships. Since then, I've always been part of small men's groups because of the value they bring. I encourage other men to join small groups where they can learn from and be accountable to each other.

Being in that first small men's group had a profound impact on my life. It helped me grow, mature, and be better prepared for the opportunities God brought my way. It gave me a solid spiritual footing, improved my relationship with my wife and kids, and made me a better employer. That experience was incredibly timely and transformative, shaping me in ways that I continue to benefit from today.

CHAPTER TWENTY-ONE

WHAT DOES A LIFE OF ADVENTURE WITH GOD LOOK LIKE?

"Never be afraid to trust an unknown future to a known God." – Corrie ten Boom

Another thing people are often surprised to learn about me is that I am a paraglider pilot. If you're not familiar with paragliding, it's when you fly with a wing-shaped parachute. You basically run off a cliff with this thing on your back and start flying. Paragliding is a fantastic adventure every time your feet leave the ground. It's very exhilarating and fun!

In order to experience the adventure of paragliding, a few things have to happen first. Number one, you have to be aware of the opportunity. You see the opportunity, then you learn about it. What is the commitment? Time, cost, risk, fears? Then you have to say yes or no. When you decide "yes" and move forward, there is an investment of time, training, and resources. Once you are properly prepared, you take off and fly, experiencing the adventure.

The adventure doesn't just happen on its own; it starts with a "yes"—a willingness to move forward and see where saying "yes" will lead you. It also takes a commitment of time and resources. For me, if I had not explored what saying "yes" to being a paragliding pilot looked like, I would have missed out on experiencing the fantastic adventure of flying!

Much like my adventures with Cathy and our mission trips, paragliding reminds me that a life of adventure with God begins with a willingness to step out in faith, make a commitment, and embrace the opportunities He places before us. Whether it's soaring through the skies or embarking on a new mission, saying "yes" to God opens the door to incredible experiences and growth.

CHAPTER TWENTY-TWO

ADVENTURES WITH CATHY: STEPPING OUT OF OUR COMFORT ZONES

"You should be courageous, not because of who you are and what you have done, but because of who God is and what He has done." – Wayne A. Mack

Cathy has been a constant support in all my endeavors, often stepping out of her comfort zone to join me in various adventures. One memorable experience was at a charity auction where Cathy surprised me with an exciting bid. I was sitting at the table with my back to her, and they were auctioning off a "fighter pilot for a day" experience. I bid a couple of times, but it quickly got too expensive for my taste. Suddenly, someone kept bidding higher and higher behind me. When I turned to see who it was, I found out it was Cathy!

The experience was at Fullerton Airport, where you fly in a tandem airplane with a Navy fighter pilot instructor. The setup was like playing laser tag in the sky. We took off from Fullerton, flew out over the ocean by Catalina Island, and did six simulated dogfights.

It was an adrenaline rush like no other, and we had an amazing time. This is just one example of Cathy's willingness to embrace my adventurous spirit.

If you recall from a story earlier in this book, I sold my Porsche to build a pastor's house in Costa Rica. Years later, I had the opportunity to buy another Porsche. A friend of mine, who is also a sports car enthusiast, suggested we take our cars to a racetrack in the desert called Chuckwalla. The experience was exhilarating. We raced on the track, focusing on improving our times rather than competing directly with others. Each lap taught us something new about handling the car better, and by the end of the day, we had covered about 100 miles on the track. The incremental improvements reminded me of how life works—continual learning and growth lead to significant progress over time.

I want to take a moment to recognize my wife's significant role in all of this. Over the years, she has made countless sacrifices so that I could pursue these incredible opportunities. While there were times we could enjoy activities together, our focus shifted after starting a family. I had more opportunities to engage in these pursuits, but Cathy's contribution is just as vital, if not more so. She created an environment where I had the necessary support and encouragement to chase after whatever God put in front of me. Every decision we made together was grounded in prayer, and she played a crucial role in those choices. None of this could have been achieved without her, absolutely.

I am deeply grateful to be in a marriage where we are spiritually aligned and share a vision for serving others in God's kingdom. Having a partner who shares this vision is crucial; Cathy's unwavering support has been invaluable. Whether by my side on adventures or holding down the fort at home during our children's early years, Cathy has been indispensable. I cannot imagine experiencing life's adventures with anyone else.

CONCLUSION

THE LEGACY OF SAYING "YES"

"He who lays up treasures on earth spends his life backing away from his treasures. To him, death is loss. He who lays up treasures in heaven looks forward to eternity; he's moving daily toward his treasures. To him, death is gain. He who spends his life moving toward his treasures has reason to rejoice." – Randy Alcorn

Reflecting on these experiences, it's clear that saying "yes" to God and investing in relationships—whether with family, friends, or colleagues—leads to incredible adventures and opportunities for growth. From family trips to professional mentorship, the consistent thread has been a commitment to live out my faith authentically and invest in the people around me. This journey of faith has not only shaped my life but also profoundly impacted those around me, demonstrating the transformative power of a life dedicated to God's principles.

The journey of saying "yes" to God is a testament to the profound impact of obedience and faith. It shows that when we align our lives with God's principles, we not only find personal fulfillment but also become conduits of His love, wisdom, and care for others. Whether through family, business, or ministry, the ripple effect of these decisions creates a legacy that honors God and enriches the lives of many.

In the end, it's not about the accolades or the tangible successes. It's about the relationships we build, the lives we touch, and the faith we live out daily. It's about being intentional with our time, proactive in our efforts, and consistent in our faith. This is the true measure of a life well-lived—a life that continually says "yes" to God's call.

You may be reading this and thinking, "I don't have this relationship with God that you are talking about, and I would like to." That is the Holy Spirit calling you to Himself. It's up to you to make the next move, to respond. It is a simple, life-changing prayer. It is the biggest "yes" to God you can say! Simply pray in your heart or out loud, "Lord Jesus, I recognize I am a sinner, and I need Your love and forgiveness. It is my desire to give my life to You and to follow You. Please help me and empower me to live a life that is honoring You. Thank You, Lord Jesus, for Your saving grace. Amen."

Congratulations if you prayed this prayer! You are embarking on a great adventure with God! The secret to a successful and fulfilling life with Christ is to daily seek Him and His Kingdom priorities and to allow the Holy Spirit to open your eyes to what He is doing around you, and join Him in His work.

ENDNOTES

CONNECT WITH MICHAEL

Thank you for taking the time to read *Say Yes to God: The Story of an Ordinary Life of Extraordinary Adventure*. If my journey has inspired or encouraged you, or if you simply want to share your own story, I would love to hear from you. Please feel free to reach out to me directly.

Email: YesGodExtraordinaryLife@gmail.com

Phone: 619.736.0233

Remember, every extraordinary adventure begins with a simple "yes" to God. Let's connect and continue this incredible journey together!

Blessings,

Michael J. Gaetke

PICTURE APPENDIX

Gaetke Family circa 1967. James, Joyce, Michael, Mark and Melody. Spring Valley, CA.

Master Carpenter/Contractor Butch Whitely and Apprentice Mike Gaetke, circa 1978.

Mike and Cathy with John Maxwell.

Mike Gaetke in Papua New Guinea, working with
Assisting Indigenous Development (AID), circa 1981.

Gaetke Family vacation and mission trip to Costa Rica, including a visit to Tabacon Hot Springs for some rest and relaxation.

Metropolitan Correctional Center (Federal Prison), San Diego, CA. Mike conducted prison ministry on the 10th and 6th floors for 10 years.

Pastor Mario's house-building team, 2010, Turrialba, Costa Rica.

Indigenous Pastor Mario with his wife Irina and their sons, 2010.

Pastor Ricauter's house-building team, Costa Rica.

Mike teaching Servant Leadership in Kenya.

Dr. Peter Mulinge, Mike Gaetke, Governor Kivutha Kibwana, Bishop Mwema, and government officials in Makueni County, Kenya.

Property dedication for the Africa Servant Leadership Institute, Makueni County, Kenya.

Home Building Project in Tijuana, Mexico, with brother-in-law Ron O'Bard.

Mountain biking adventure at Mammoth Mountain, CA.

Left to Right: Emily, Margot, David, Cathy, Eloise, Mike, Nicole, Paul

Amazon Rainforest, Brazil.

2024 Graduation Ceremony, Africa Servant
Leadership Development Institute, Makueni, Kenya.

Mike launching for a paragliding flight in the French Alps

ACKNOWLEDGEMENTS

I would like to thank my wife, Cathy, for her encouragement and support throughout this book project. Without her urging to move forward, this book would not have been written! I am also grateful for her support over the 40 years of our marriage and for our partnership in living an ordinary life full of adventure. I would like to thank my mom and dad, James and Joyce, for giving me a firsthand view of what it looks like to live an authentic Christian life. I would also like to acknowledge the ministry partners around the world with whom I have had the privilege to work. Additionally, I want to extend my gratitude to the exceptional team at Goodwill Media, especially Emily Loomis and Carl Dobrowolski.

BIBLIOGRAPHY

Gaetke, Michael. Say Yes to God: The Story of an Ordinary Life of Extraordinary Adventure.

Scripture References:

- 2 Timothy 1:7 (NIV): "For the Spirit God gave us does not make us timid, but gives us power, love and self-discipline."

- James 1:5 (NIV): "If any of you lacks wisdom, you should ask God, who gives generously to all without finding fault, and it will be given to you."

- Colossians 3:23 (NKJV): "And whatever you do, do it heartily, as to the Lord and not to men."

- Exodus 3:1-4:17 (NIV): The call of Moses and the burning bush.

- Luke 1:26-38 (NIV): The Annunciation to Mary.

- 1 Samuel 16:1-13, 17:1-50 (NIV): The anointing of David and his battle with Goliath.

- Acts 9:1-19 (NIV): The conversion of Saul to Paul.

Books and Authors:

- Covey, Stephen R. The 7 Habits of Highly Effective People.

- Covey, Sean. The 7 Habits of Highly Effective Teens.

- Carnegie, Dale. How to Win Friends and Influence People.

- Foster, Richard J. Celebration of Discipline.

Online Sources:

- Maxwell, John. "Servant Leadership Archives - John Maxwell." Accessed July 20, 2024. https://www.johnmaxwell.com/blog/category/servant-leadership.

- Maxwell, John. "Live2Lead: A Chance to Serve Your People and Your Community." Accessed July 20, 2024. https://www.johnmaxwell.com/blog/live2lead-a-chance-to-serve-your-people-and-your-community.

- Servant Leadership Institute. "Principles of Servant Leadership." Accessed July 20, 2024. https://www.servantleadershipinstitute.com/.

- Maxwell, John. "The 5 Key Resilience Traits You Need Right Now." Accessed July 20, 2024. https://www.johnmaxwell.com/blog/the-5-key-resilience-traits-you-need-right-now.

- Maxwell, John. "Does Love Work as a Leadership Principle?" Accessed July 20, 2024. https://www.johnmaxwell.com/blog/does-love-work-as-a-leadership-principle.

ENDORSEMENT

"In Say Yes to God, Michael Gaetke shares an extraordinary journey that beautifully illustrates the power of faith and servant leadership. His life experiences are a testament to what God can do through someone willing to say 'yes.' This book is a must-read for anyone looking to deepen their faith and make a meaningful impact."

— John C. Maxwell

www.ingramcontent.com/pod-product-compliance
Lightning Source LLC
Chambersburg PA
CBHW070724130626
46553CB00005B/2140